Counting Backwards Rhyming Fun
Twenty-five to None

Story and Illustrations by Cheryl Jackson Giles

JACC Collection LLC
6375 Penn Avenue Suite B #1059
Pittsburgh, Pennsylvania 15206

This book is for all children who are learning to count backwards.

25, 24

Twenty-five, twenty-four.
Let's skip out the door.

23, 22

Twenty-three, twenty-two.
This gift is for you.

21, 20

Twenty-one, twenty.
It tastes so minty.

Pucker up to our...
Natural Mint Lemonade

19, 18

Nineteen, eighteen.
I take my sister skating.

17, 16

Seventeen, sixteen.
We like to go fishing.

15, 14

Fifteen, fourteen.
We dress for Halloween.

13, 12

Thirteen, twelve.
Can you hear the church
bells?

11, 10

Eleven, ten.
Get him from the
playpen.

9, 8

Nine, eight.
Look who's at the gate.

7, 6

Seven, six.
The drawer really sticks.

5, 4

Five, four.
Let's run to Cee's store.

Cee's
STORE
Frozen Fruit
Pops

3, 2

Three, two.
Can I help you?

1, 0

One, zero.
You're my hero!

YOU'RE MY HERO
Paste cutout drawing, color page, or photograph of your favorite hero here.

Draw, color, or paste a photograph of your hero inside of the white space on the next page. Ask an adult to help you cut out the picture along the dotted lines then paste it on top of the One, Zero you're my hero page.

Cut here

Another story by
Cheryl Jackson Giles

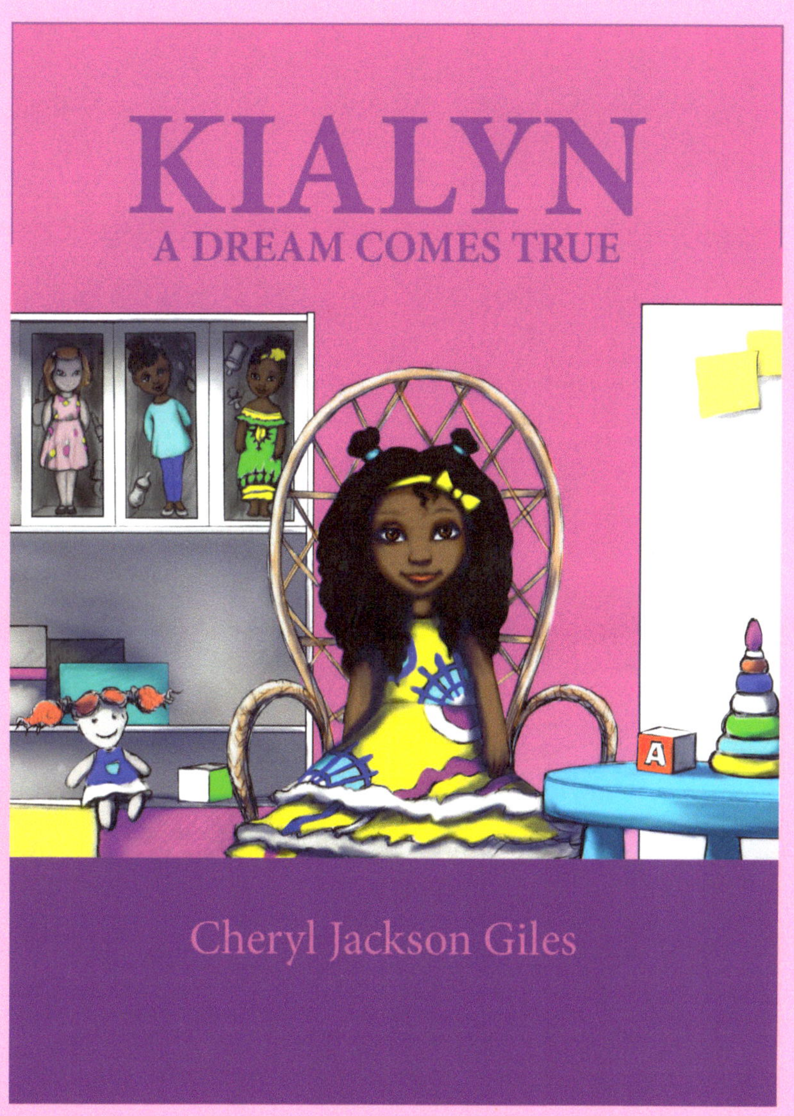

KIALYN
A DREAM COMES TRUE

Cheryl Jackson Giles